Prophesying the Past

NOEL KING

7th June 2010

For Julie

with great memories
of past trips and
future ones,

Noel K

salmonpoetry

Published in 2010 by
Salmon Poetry
Cliffs of Moher, County Clare, Ireland
Website: www.salmonpoetry.com
Email: info@salmonpoetry.com

ISBN 978-1-907056-46-8

Cover artwork: *"Ghosts" by Anne-Marie Glasheen – www.glasheen.co.uk*
Cover design & typesetting: *Siobhán Hutson*
Printed in England by imprint*digital*.net

Published with financial assistance from the Arts Council

in memory of the grandparents

Maud & Tom Hennebery

Bridget & Tommy King

Acknowledgements

Acknowledgement is due to the editors of the following print publications where these poems or versions of them first appeared:

IRELAND: *A Sense Of Cork; Black Mountain Review; Books Ireland; Boyne Berries; Cathal Buí Summer School Anthology; Census; Cork Literary Review; Cyphers; Cúm; The Edgeworth Papers; Heart Of Kerry; Irish Medical Journal; The Kerryman; The Lantern Review; Markings – The Galway Advertiser; Microphone On; New Series: Departures; Poetry Ireland Review; Real Imaginings; Revival; Riposte; The SHop; Southword; The Stony Thursday Book; Studies; The Sunday Tribune; Wildeside.*

INTERNATIONAL: *A Bard Hair Day* (England); *Aural Images* (England); *Bongos of the World* (Japan); *Brittle Star* (England); *Canopy* (India); *Christian Poetry Review* (Isle of Lewis); *Coke Fish* (USA); *The Dalhousie Review* (Canada); *Eclipse* (England); *Face The Music* (England); *Family History Monthly* (England); *The Flagburner* (Finland); *Freefall* (Canada); *FreeXpression* (Australia); *Fresh* (New Zealand); *Green's Magazine* (Canada); *Image Nation* (England); *The Indian Book Chronicle* (India); *Intermezzo* (Germany); *Jamm* (New Zealand); *The Journal* (England); *Kotaz* (South Africa); *Labour Of Love* (Canada); *Links* (England); *Lit Speak* (Germany); *Lunatic Chameleon* (Canada); *Mandakini* (India); *The Mawaheb International* (Canada); *Micropress* (New Zealand); *The Nashwaak Review* (Canada); *New England Review* (Australia); *New Leaf* (Germany); *The New Orphic Review* (Canada); *"O"* (Nepal); *Orbis* (England); *Peace & Freedom* (England); *Poems, Proses & Other Assorted Goodies* (Malaysia); *The Poet Tree* (England); *Poetry Salzburg Review* (Austria); *Polestar Writers' Journal* (Australia); *Pulsar* (England); *Quadrant* (Australia); *Quantum Leap* (England); *Rattappallax* (USA); *Read the Music* (England); *Shine* (India); *Social Alternatives* (Australia); *Staple* (England); *Stardust Memories* (Holland); *Studio – a Journal of Christian's Writing* (Australia); *Tickled by Thunder* (Canada); *Triveni* (India); *You Dancin'?* (Finland); *Words Unbound/Mots Déchaînés* (France).

Black and Tan and *Old Silver* were published on-line in Tryst (USA), www.tryst3.com

Contents

A Mother's Watch

Door ajar, I hear his tears.
Sitting on his side of their bed,
his workman's fingers winding

the watch that he bought her,
that came off for the washing-up;
that was always five minutes fast.

She gave us the gift
of that extra five minutes
always,
for school,
for trains back to college;
everything.

Now it's wound
he hands it over
to me.

On Christmas Morning

my father's father is bounding across his farm.
Three small heads follow, having brought the gifts
of the Magi to less fortunates, short-cutted by their own fields.
The patriarch ignores the bulk of poles
the country has erected on his land,
though he is grateful for the electric in his home.

Santa Claus was able to turn on the kitchen light
and see where everything went last night;
coming to the younger ones: a boy trotting here now,
and a girl at home with mother making Christmas.
Outside this morning, after presents, and looking skywards,
the children sent a prayer to take him safe to the North Pole.

This evening all will milk cows and break bread
into little pieces for birds in the cold.
But the family will go to Mass next
where children will whisper
of the wonders of the man in the red suit.

My father's mother will raise the window sash
any moment now and her husband will see again
across a love grown in them.
She will call a greeting, wave
and years away their children will remember
Christmas.

Black and Tan

My grandmother knew the opening scrape
of her front gate was not a friend,
told us she remembered staying perfectly still,
his hard steps crunching through her.

She didn't remember his face,
how long he stood in her kitchen,
what lies or truths she uttered
while my infant aunt gurgled in her cot.

She did remember his words:
I have a little girl like this at home, myself.

For sixty-three years she stepped over
the spot on her flagged floor
where the Black and Tan had stood.

The Letter

I hold a letter my grandfather wrote;
it was found in an attic by the daughter
of a woman he wrote to:

April 3rd, 1947, Castlegregory, County Kerry –
he didn't live there, was on holiday.
His wife, my uncles and mother,

probably cavorted on the sea-shore
as he scribbled in secret
to this woman he kept from everyone;

probably saw only a few times a year
when his company called their conferences,
AGMs, branch managers' meetings and things

at the H.Q. in Dublin city, where he might have
rented a room for her to come to him
after finishing work in her Civil Service job,

pretending to the landlady she was his wife.
They might have dined and danced
and made love all night, perhaps not, I don't know;

all I know is the tickles of skin upon skin
and scribbles of dark blue ink
have – years after his death – found him out.

It might have been all innocent
and they slept alone, an intelligent like-minds
thing, but the letter has great passion,

he calls her *my love* – while Granny slept
by him and cooked and cleaned
for him and reared his children with him.

The letter says he's ice-packed a salmon,
caught with his own hands,
and is sending the runner-boy at the factory

to put it on the train. He wishes she could fish
beside him some day, maybe some day...
expresses shock that the Russians

are blocking Ireland's entry to the UN
because of de Valera's war-time
sympathy with the Axis Powers

and Franco's Spain. He hopes
the landlady at her digs has recovered,
would not after all have to sell up,

letting her tenants of so many
years to find new places to live.
The woman's daughter and I

plan to meet, muse upon the secret,
wonder why more letters don't exist.
Maybe his love destroyed them near her end,

that it broke her heart to burn them all
and missed this one. I'm not telling
my wife, anyone, that I am having this

meeting in Dublin, will share the secret
of this tryst with my Grandad,
take it to my own grave.

Holiday by the Sea

A black bin liner
bursts in the sand dune.

After their mother died
on a caravan holiday
at a Kerry seaside,
the family stuffed her stuff
and left it there,
while her blue print dress
bought in Penneys for the holiday
coloured her remains and the sun
scorched the coffin on the roof rack
of the family car going back to the city
– this the only sunshine
the family saw the whole two weeks.

One of the children had run to her Daddy:
Nana, Nana, falled down, down on the beach.
She died in her son's arms,
the sea breezes ruffling her hairdo,
spreading a purple hue across her face.

After the funeral in Dublin,
after the children returned to school,
winter came,
rain fell on her grave

and in a high tide
the sea claimed her remnants from the bin liner:
bras, knickers, cardigans, slacks, green wellington boots,
Fox's Glacier Mints seeping through their wrappers,
slips, slippers, tights, sandals,
and the Bible and rosary beads she clasped
at Sunday Mass in Castlegregory
where the priest welcomed all holidaymakers,
                              wishing them a safe journey home.

The 20B

The man on the back of the bus takes a Siberian kite
out of his satchel, all grey and white
and dark. He plays with it today.

Yesterday, there was nothing unusual about
him at all, kite on lap, he just stared out the window.

On Wednesday he was humming to himself
some chant in a strange language.

The day before that he hand-rolled
cigarette after cigarette and smoked
incessantly: it's like that upstairs on
the 20B   driver too scared   ignores it.

On Monday, I can't remember,
perhaps he had his eyes closed.

Our stop   and on the steps
he lets it go high into the air,
more vibrant than any bright-coloured kites
we Irish might have.

Turf

I

Hay-knife skims through topsoil,
my father slices through the bank,
knowing the sound of a good sod.
Above him I check-prod each with a pike,
an eye on one side to the faraway forest,
another to the road and our tea inside the car.
There is no talk, just the knowing
of work, fire for winter warmth.
With a pike prong I write T H E B E AT L E S
– one letter each to ten wet sods,
on an eleventh I draw a little drum-kit with my penknife,
vow to keep them together, a kind of souvenir
to show my girlfriend; burn in a winter ritual.
Getting to the white clay, we go back up,
slit another section to cut down again.
My radio moves with me. He closes his ears
– pop music an easy cross to bear
for teen-help in the bog.
Having a slash behind last year's rick,
I watch where the wind blows – can't wet the turf.
Ten minutes after the town's Angelus bell,
midges scream to our bodies,
using their evening's prowess to send us home
to burn last year's stash, and fizzle
the rhythm of our work with Radox baths.

II

We turn every sod
for the other side to dry;
man-spits on palms every so often
to keep the pike-grip.
I am on tiptoes,
chastised for not making enough space
between the rows for walking-working.
We have girls in the bog this time,
sisters for the easy work. I instruct.
I don't know that they know I'm proud
'til I spot our Daddy's smile.
I search for T H E   B E A T L E S,
but they've been broken up.

III

Then we 'foot' it – the worst part, backs bent;
a circle of sods support each other
with another on top.
We sprinkle on sops of hay
before making the V shape stack I stack.

It rains for home, drenched-wet-sweat
now dried into us by the breeze.
Dad showers upstairs, I downstairs.
My sister dries her hair at the fireplace
with eyes on the television set;
Something (in the way she moves)
being danced to on Top of the Pops.
The fire warms the Pieta replica on the mantelpiece.

IV

We should load today but it's not set yet.
Muttering curses at the rainfall of the week,
my father throws his hands about,
but never to the God-sky,
chats with a passer-by bog dealer
the same complaints of their fathers before them.
Me and my girl home from the pictures
earlier than everyone else on Saturday night,
put on the Sgt. Pepper album, then back to Revolver.
She, a town girl, asks me to wash my hands
before returning them to her lace covered breasts
after adding another sod to the fire.

V

We never found anything exciting
as people in bogs say they do:
no bones, no earthenware, no coins, no treasure.
At last loading, we hire an important looking van
and bend, gather, rise, throw,
bend, gather, rise, throw.
I am still searching for any remaining sod
of T H E   B E A T L E S.

Hay Fever

In memory of Paddy King

The hay turned to stone that summer
as virgin ground got cracked
by heavy machinery we followed;
where stones lay we reached and picked,

reached and picked on dull days,
loading endless trailers.
I asked if a machine existed to pick,
the men shut me up, whispered our redundancy.

Our relief was the landowner's beck for the break.
The men's faces tried my pace,
I, not rushing to another field
to reach plastic orange-crush containers
into a clear stream. I made tea of it,
the land-water tea was special,
as the smell of smoking men,
their cigarettes' harm sucked away by the breeze.

My raw-hot hands were soothed by a first love,
first money affording 'the pictures'
where I kept nodding to sleep. She wanted
to come to the meadow, I fumbled to explain
that the men didn't take their women there.

This memory doesn't include sunshine,
just the sun in the heart of bursting back
from nature what she
had quietly taken.

The land stands enriched.

An Irish Father. New York. Spring.

I think I'll move here... after my finals.
Her words shock him. His baby girl
is downing Coca Cola in Central Park.
...funny, she says, with a hint of American,
it tastes better here.

Her older brothers
read their father,
do not speak
of their exile here.

The father plucks
a blade of grass, longs
to compare the colour
but crushes it back in his fist.

The daughter's eyes are spanning the skyline.

Wrists

As once I held
your wrist
between thumb
and forefinger
and they could close
round with room
to spare; yours

is double mine
now I long, even
once, to press
my thumb into
that cavity, find
your pulse and
you'll know a heart
breaks for you.

Dinner

Pained by peeling
shrivelled mushrooms
he sets his home-face
light-bright.
She waits, impatient
with chopped onions
to mush with the fungi,
frizzle on a non-stick pan,
the surface long scratched away.
They eat with silence.

Grand-Aunts

are taking tea in Heaven;
chirping about what happens
down below, the way young ones
these days carry on –
have the child,
buy the house,
live in sin   all before
                getting married.

The maiden aunts miss
the scones with thick butter and jam
and the nice tea sets each of them had;
sets that went to their nieces,
heirlooms slowly cracked and broken,
one lot pawned to a broker,
another sold to an antique dealer for a fraction
and one at auction on eBay.

One single niece
keeps a pride service as carefully
as she can. Each time she breaks one
she thinks that that grand-aunt will feel
the crack in her bones, but though the grand-aunt can see,
she doesn't mind, smiling that the woman
down below hasn't yet discovered the glued together bits
on the dinner plate at the back of the set.

Home-making

My uncle took his bride
from the portals of an Indian summer
of print dresses and cream ice cream.

Her aunts worked together a patchwork quilt;
her mother's delft – unbroken for two generations –
went on a clevvy her handyman father made.

My uncle made handiwork of her
home-making, drank to a busy grave.

Now in *this* Indian summer
she trusts the weather,
washes the quilt,

sits on the terrace, a newspaper,
glasses unsteady on her apron-lap,
watching it dry.

They Made the Sound of Her Man

She kept his wellington boots,
under her bed, uncleaned, dusty,
since being removed from his body,
blood stains fading from the wounds
where the bull gouged him.

She kept no lock of hair, or his pipes,
nothing but the wellingtons
and wedding photo on the mantle.

Horns plunged through his groin,
stomach and chest, hooves smashed his face
before the bull casually strolled off to shag another cow;
  his own bull he had raised from a calf,
  his own bull who turned on him one hot August day
  in an uncautious moment when he was dog-less in the field.

The neighbour who found him,
found a piece of his penis on the grass
but hid it in his pocket from the wife.

After the funeral,
the bull slaughtered,
the herd sold,
she slipped the boots under the bed
before undressing and sleeping overhead.

The wellies told her he was close,
she heard his clopping in them before his face appeared for meals,
he pulled them off only before climbing into bed
beside her every night when he made love to her
every night and again every morning.

They made the sound of her man,
they made the sound of her man.

Pizza Girl

On my third visit she gave a first smile
to me, with the pizza. She pulled off
a latex glove to take my cash, ring it in, give change.
I tried a touch of her fingertips, but she was professional,
I liked that, but why'd she work
in a shit place like this?

On my fourth visit I asked for a Moonfaced
one, 'cause my son was on a visit to me.
She looked at me peculiar,
sniggered, suggested I edit a piece
out myself, then I'd have a Moonfaced.

Knowing my boy didn't like olives,
I pushed them with my fingers
to one side. While we ate
he told me of his mother and school.
I just thought of my pizza girl.

She short cutted the park
while I pushed the boy on a swing; it flew back, hit me,
as I watched her tight arse along the distance.
Jesus Christ, my balls…! My lad laughed. I flushed.
Daddy got his goolies caught with the swing,
watchin' women in the park,
he'd tell his mother later on, the little fart.

All summer long I tried the entire menu,
finding new combinations,
using my credit card even for a $4.99 meal
– 'cause she handed me a pen to sign my name.

By September she had left the job.
The new girl would only take regular orders
and anyway she wasn't half as nice.

Herself at Fifty

I

With husband at sport,
she changes into walking shoes,
leaves the washing to dry,
heads to hills now accustomed to her hike:
waters them with tears.
She feels the canopy of
her favourite tree,
a redundant gate,
a hidden shell of a shed,
before the time comes
to face her front door again.

II

Her lightness flatters the grass mainly in summer
and on dry autumn afternoons,
but in winter only on Saturdays
when the family are at their thing.
She touches the hard iron
of a secluded gate she leans on,
has never pushed open
or wondered which farmer owns this field;
takes only thoughts from his grass, his sky, his herd.
She smiles at thinking
the farmer should get royalties
for poems taken from his land.
Here her heart stakes to sounds
that present themselves
in moments that shape the sense
of parts of those close to her.
Here is the resting place for
      her thoughts,
      her muse,
      and her God.

Naked Mountain

It is not even Epiphany yet but the heathered boreen beckons
towards the mountain where an altar was laid; has lain since
the tradition started sometime in the night-time of 1950s Ireland.

All the small boys and I were marched in November squelch;
made go to pray every day, Sundays with our fathers,
and the mothers weekdays, mine and the neighbours' above us by

two-hundred-and-two-feet, leaving behind younger squabbling
children, animals milked and fed, sinks full of warm dishes,
the instructions of the weather forecast

and the body that said it was too tired to go climbing. Rosary
beads clasped in home-knit mitts, the breezes ruddying cheeks,
until we reached the altar that a bolt of lightning had split in two.

Today, is my return journey and I climb to pray;
past the derelict that was our house,
past the barking dogs of the people who live

where our neighbours did, two-hundred-and-two feet above us,
try to show the hounds I'm no stranger; climb and find the altar,
touch it, place a flower I've brought from the city and remember.

After Their Boy Leaves Home

Joe insists the lad's Airfix Models remain hanging,
but gives away the tired-out vinyl records,
the turntable going to a nephew just getting his teens.

Mary washes his left-behind clothes,
doles them by:
                    unworn to her nephews,
                    worn to Oxfam,
                    well-worn to a recycling bin.
                    Three underpants become dusters.

In his playhouse in the garden
                    he'd hidden child colours with black paint;
                    sat, head bent, under the low ceiling
                    plucking guitar chords.

Joe bursts the roof,
                    hinges it,
                    creosotes it;
                    makes a fuel shed.

Mary misses most the sounds
                    from the mini-amp through her kitchen window.
                    It's out of place in the porch, waiting
                    for enquiries to an ad in the local paper.

He'll buy a better model
                    when he gets his feet in London, he says,
                    and promises, swears to them
                    he'll never busk on the Underground.

Face Up

At the art centre
you sit for this girl
who studies your face,
feels you through your pores.
You talk about yourself
as you did yesterday and the day before
while she draws you as you will look
a quarter-of-a-century from now.

The this she presents will be you
in twenty-five-years, it's where you're dancing to
through the race-work and back, work and back
home, where your wife admires her new furniture,
looks at programmes on the TV, gets notions about things.

There's another twenty-five by fifty-two carving Sunday lunches
for whatever few family are around,
and switching from the World Service to Lyric FM and back.
You begin to realise   that all there is   is art.

Facing a Skip

In the middle of the move
I try to scrap things
I know I would use again,
weigh the consequences
of what you hit me with:
  tool bits,
  hinges,
  old bills,
  negatives never to be reprinted,
  broken clocks;
  yes, useful things
  – I was damn handy around the house.
I write my new place address
  for the removal man,
  telling him I'll follow
  by car with the last
  of my bits and pieces.
You left a window open this morning
– this morning before going golfing –
a window I inserted myself
with you holding the frame in place
while I drilled in my marks.
I leave my marks everywhere here, my love.

The Bass Fish

Casting out I hope for a bass
'cause this evenin' a woman's comin'
and I'm cookin'. She lifts something
in my heart. She's new to these parts
which is why I want to catch the bass,
to thrill some aphrodisiacal mood; I hope
maybe 'twill make her want for me
and wish for me, and if she wants a man
there aren't too many in the village
and none of 'em can fish like I can.
I cast afresh, awaiting a bass,
smile to meself at our chats in the pub.
So far she's mighty interestin', details the life
she used to live in a shitty city.
I laugh with my final cast – long for a bass;
I'll never do what her husband used to,
going to the supermarket to fish, on pay day,
stupid man – wonders now why she left,
which is just my luck   just my luck.

Rush Hour on the Underground

Cities make men dream each other
into worlds they never claim,
lives that can be tossed up and broken
in the fields of a dream's wish.

Husband

I will not grieve for her deity.
I will grieve for old courtship,
the then freshness, the giving in;
births of our children.

I will not grieve for sallow, sullen
suppers where food was good
but voice was stern: a bitter-footed
wake of a woman pleasuring
in tantrum-riddling her closest.

I will grieve for times when
on my arm she got gracious
to others, smiled to menfolk
on racecourses, her knowledge
of the nags sometimes bettering theirs;
and her style, clothes I liked her in,
designs from my success.

I will not grieve for her begrudging
my interests – the screaming
at my I'll-be-a-bit-late-home calls, the waiting,
cocooned in our smoke-filled bedroom,
to spit at whatever I'd been at.

I will grieve for our children,
losing a mother in their young adulthood,
a mother they could rely on but
never predict a sharp or soft response,
or which, from the mood of the day.

I will not grieve for the sagging breasts,
shapeless lines of a smoking woman's
later-life body, especially when
he who sees remembers: a hard frozen
1950s Doris Day swimsuit on a local beach.

I will grieve for years when
package holidays got oftener, lavisher,
then more lavish but less satisfying.

I will not grieve for the first trip without the children
when she went topless
and my shame thinking other men
were peering at my wife's tits,
taking pity on what was mine.

I will grieve for moments
of close time in the bed or the kitchen perhaps,
or a quickie somewhere,
where the soft-voiced one I had fallen in love with
still enchanted in me.

I will touch her now, soon,
one last time, kiss the coldness away,
shoulder her with my children,
and the people that know us
will shake our hands,
embrace,
mutter,
grieve briefly with us.

I will not grieve for her deity.

Thank You for the Music

We are death-clearing
our parents' home.

In the garage one white key
off our piano
turns up.
My sister goes white:
Why did he break it up?

I find a black key in the garden,
rotted and chewed
by a dog or something.

My sibling shivers
finding an antique piano leg
propping a fuel-shed worktop:
He told us he'd sold it!

Da hated the piano,
wanted me to football
not have Mam make us learn.

Now I cry.
My sister too.
We hold each other.

Father's Second Wife

To explain the new marriage he silently offered me
a box of Kodak snaps, punched my cheek fondly
before checking my farm work. She
made tea, untied a parcel of sticky buns,

smiled weakly at me. You were photographed in
a costume of pseudo-Spanish flamenco – or some
country – a honeymoon you'd just had with my father,
the costume playing games – as the sun does – with him.

You changed my mother's house for the sake of it,
made sickly colours in the place, had him carpenter it
into new shapes. I resented helping, holding,
knuckles white on white timber presses he screwed in

– nights he screwed you in my mother's bed. Through
the window I caught you baking bread, throwing
the dough on the wood table and making momentary
phallic shapes, pressing, kneading, flattening them,

crafting ring-bread – at tea time I said I wasn't hungry.
You took up with me after my father's stroke, when he
could stoke you no more. We watched The Hardy Boy
Mysteries and The Nancy Drew Mysteries together

on alternative Mondays. The Nancy ones proved to you I
wasn't a nancy boy. Then your sly, pun-intended comment
on The Hardy Boys and we were off; my father, oblivious,
out on the terrace, a car rug covering

the equipment he no longer had. We got – or you got –
more daring in time; doing me while he
was in the house, and eventually with him
in the same room, too senile to notice.

All of This

for the Flynn Sisters

In Sydney
        she takes a poetry book
        from the An Post mailer
        and wonders
about this sister,
insignificant little thing
left behind when
        they emigrated after their wedding;
        remembers
the face in the gang,
shy throwing of confetti
clinging to Mom or was it Dad?;
that flower girl   whose face
said nothing but later grew
into the woman who
became the poet who
wrote about
all of this.

Mrs

Your gold band
has not expanded,

contracted, since
that day
it was placed with love.

An aunt's linen present
has threaded
but you've reworked it,
creating cushion covers,
dishcloths.

Daily cleaning for him,
washing for him,
feeding him,
giving yourself to him,
took you

to a hospital bed:
you grasp your ring,
try to roll it round;
a mannerism
you picked up
after marriage.

My Grandmother at War, 1944

You begin to suffer rations gladly
to suffer for those who are suffering worse;

to each their own tea jar, sugar jar.
Your boys pull beetroot from the vegetable garden,

you don't skin them, just snip tops and bottoms,
plunge into boiling water. You can no longer afford

the cleaning girl once a week but keep her on anyway,
for her mother's sake and a cousin of hers

could be at The Front right now.
Here is no tableau of peacefulness,

knowing people who know people who know people gone.
A young man you met at a turn on the floor

in a great house party gets killed.
Your husband still plays his part:

talking senselessness with other men,
helping the rations with extra fists of grain

to favoured neighbours, blind-eyeing townspeople
who rob a head of cabbage

or a stick of a carrot from his tilled garden.
Preparing for back-to-school, you shear

your four sons' blonde heads, thank God they
are so young, that in Kerry you are so far away from war.

You want your man to stop the daily newspaper
your sons pore over on the weaves and turns

of your kitchen table, making their play glamour battles
in fading after-school sun. Your girls tell your boys

they're silly digging trenches and shooting
stick-pistols at each other,

but their father claims all this natural
in peace or war. You scour the table

to shrieking sounds of guerrilla warfare,
and call them in for their tea.

Fisherman

He had left her at home
waiting to cook a salmon supper
                    or a trout.
Since his stroke
he couldn't steady the hooks,
often sliced finger skin.
Another fisherman found him
slumped at the footbridge;
                    alerted the wife.
Her hands went straight
for an antiseptic
as if to soothe his cuts.
The scales of fish clinging,
the smell of the river lingering.

N.I., GI, 1943

When the GIs arrived,
de Valera, worried
for the virtue of Northern girls,
angrily asked why United States of America
hadn't sought permission.

Meanwhile, the men
– some of them even black men –
copulated in pre-Rural Electrification bushes.
The women had never known
such excitement in their dry lives.

But the war was nearly over and soon
only a sheen of sweat remained.
Fathers, mothers and de Valera wiped their brows
and slapped their own backs again
for Mother Ireland's great sense of hospitality.

Fortress

I upturn boxes of matches
onto the workbench,
press them together
glueing an even row:
                    becomes a wall,
                    a square becomes
                    a building over days
                    becomes a castle.
I scatter plastic soldiers,
click a box camera,
before seven-year-old eyes dull.
Bored fingers crack a match:
                    malicious eyes
                    burn and stare
                    through the inferno
at a single green soldier
melting inside
as shutter after shutter
exposes   closes   exposes   closes.

Seminary, 1966

They walk,
a regiment to their God,
chosen for His new flock,
marching like schoolchildren,
a tarmac straight by trees
that shelter shadows of past priests.

They halt
at the silver gates,
spy the other world.
Their leader stones his face,
vows eyes downward,
crosses them to devotions in the cathedral.
Here is training,
watching virtue,
glory gloved by a white collar.

The boys see their altar.

The street has shut
but it threads a world
that haunts them in vespers,
whispers a World Cup
on black & white television sets
people in that-sex-world see.
Envied England wins.

They know
physical is mandatory here,
to regiment games,
exercises, swims.
Some keep passion inside,
pray to Him
for endless vocation.

Air Force Sweethearts

They
  flew
    into
      the
        girls
          in
            advance
              of
                marriage,
                  no
                    other
                      time
                        a
                        better
                          excuse
                          than
                            war-time.
                          If I am killed
                            my love,
                        at least we'll have
                        had each other.
              But in
                the pilot's
                    head:
                my child will live on,
                she'll be grateful having it,
                my child will live on...
nothing;
      a hungry bastard.
                    The
                    girls
                    were
                    left
                    broken
                    hearted
                    too.

Planting, 1955

The trees are sturdy now. In your youth and courting
a neighbour-farmer's daughter, you chose your spot,
had a word with your parents, got the blessing to build.

But first you planted, beyond the haggard, away
from your parents' privacy, a myriad of beech and birch
and fruit – several varieties your mother advised you needed –

and oak for your grandchildren; trees a woman could look out to,
admire colour in four seasons, trees that shed at different times.
The first blossoms shot out for your bride to come home to.

They grew fruit as your fruit grew up under them, climbed them,
plucked the apples, pears and plums, and underneath, gooseberry
bushes that kept the herd away from the lawn. Your offspring built

hideouts and tree houses, cut branches to build go-karts,
concoctions of wheelie things, inventors' things, playtime things.
When the kitchen drew dark you gave in to nagging and nipped

and cut, your sons helping some of the higher reaches,
your daughters delighting in shouting *TIMBER* down below.
Still there were threats of lightning, but thank God and please

God it has not struck. Now, after you have been lowered
into the same Mother Earth that grew them,
we stand under your trees; drink, smoke, nibble sandwiches,

reminisce, laugh and cry; your children waking you.

The Men's Ward

In a bed of hygienic-white
he stares ahead at the past.
Bright nurses feed, shave, pill-pop him.
He tries to put his mind away
when they strip him,
the tinkle of potency disgusting him.

People come: children
with tales of their living lives,
grapes and day-old newspapers.
They wait,
while he stares
back at the future.

Sleeping Quarters

I count sheep to the rhythm
of breath from your frame
in the soft bed as I twist on
dishevelled cushions on the floor.
How do you sleep?
Which dreams go?
Which aren't allowed in
your complex brain that figures
the eventual balance of everything?

My breaths are sharp, hollow,
as I stutter into a soft sleep,
dream of a journey without clocks
to an unnamed mountain top
where winds whisk wisps of your hair,
but you have no wild abandon
and lead me down the marked route.

When I wake it's to chinks
of light in worn, purple curtains
and you stretching, smiling at me
and enquiring if I've slept well.

Listen, and you will hear the sea

Her sideboard held
two proud shells –
my grandfather's bounty
from the only days apart
in their fifty-seven years –
the edges clipped,
but sounds intact.

Her eyes beamed care
into my hands
any time I picked them up
and I did at will;
one to each ear,
imagining the beach I knew
that she knew, the beach that, at eighty-nine,
she could no longer take me to.

I sprayed on furniture polish
one Christmas clean – she rebuked gently,
showing how, wiping the grooves with a flannel.

If I could pick them up today,
I would hear as vivid,
but I don't need to.

At School on the Death of Frost, 1963

In memory of Bryan Mac Mahon

...today, boys, is a sad day. We have lost
another master. We will read him again,
but can no longer wonder letters to him
for his meanings. Today we will celebrate
his life and compose an elegy.

Poetry is free, our master says.
You can take your inkwells
outside if you want, but boys who do
better have something after the twenty minutes.
From the class back I wonder my elegy,
its moments and meanings
for that poet with the cold name.

Faces tried to find spaces
others weren't searching in,
the air limit of the classroom
making us question this 'muse power':
I mean, Jesus, She can't get through to all of us!

Our master
kept his face down at his desk,
didn't quaffle the messin'.

He's sad for Frost. D'you think he knew him well?

The fella in my poem tore himself
with a saw and bled and died,
we leave when his father finds him,
dies too with shock
and mourners flock over a hill.

I never kept it,
even though us boys knew
poetry was a man's game.

Watercolour Christmas

It was almost Christmas Eve
when you went to snip holly, cut the tree.
I, the last child waited, frustrated,
impatient to decorate the house as you
and your forefathers had done.

Holly was barren that year.
That frightened you, a sign of things,
you said you'd never seen it without berries.
I asked why the trees were so quiet this year?
And what holly stood for?
It's an old custom, you said.
It hit me that, although aged, you didn't know everything.

I placed it to hide high spots
where faded biscuit tins with fishing gear emerged
and cardboard boxes kept batteries
and cartridges warm until spring.

I took tiny beads, dunked my fingers
in watercolour red, dried them on newspaper
under my bed; glued them on the holly branches.
Look Grandad, look, we found some with berries.

Visitors admired my holly too,
marvelled at how we'd found it.
That Christmas night one bead popped
to the floor, then another and another.
I, red faced, said: *Sure, aren't all decorations false nowadays.*
They all just laughed.

Cape Cod, 1969

She smiles nicely at the black officer
sweating a cap on the road junction
three miles before the Kennedy summer residence,
Sorry, Ma'am, he says politely to her Irish request.
Her American son reverses his bonnet-goes-on-forever car,
finds the mountain from where, the guard said,
if you see someon' swimmin', it'll be them:
the Kennedys.
She roots herself briefly to this part on the Atlantic coastline,
where the dream family of her own family name
risk in warmer waters than hers.

     Her eyes moisten a second
     meeting her son's.

         He has joined America.
         He'll hold this moment
         in his Pontiac car:
              his Mamma here,
              her new hairdo,
              the awe on her face.
              In the back seat
              his wife re-does her lipstick,
              his Dadda lights another cigarette.

Old Silver

Her cup has been stolen again.
Last time she'd been lucky,
the police found it in a ditch
on a neighbouring farm.

If the silver turns up this time,
her family can no longer enjoy
its sheen, her story repeats:

being the only woman
on the team that rowed
to victory – August 11th, 1928.

Her taut arms have softened and hardened,
pink lips whitened. She's dead.
The crack-man rows to new prey.

Counterparts

for the newborn of Chernobyl

At seven months
I am wearing a white sticker
for her in the other corner.
In seven years
I will, God willing,
still wear it, when she
is in her new world.
At fourteen
I will understand why I wore it,
anger, fear will rise inside me.
At twenty-one,
I might take up her cause
or may not care
or maybe somebody,
in another corner,
will be holding a flag day
for me.

Only People in Towns Think the Country is a Peaceful Place

The
drive
into
town
is
particularly
hazardous
when
the
tide
is
in. We get looked down at in town as we watch our homing time.

The
air
is
tough
to
take
here
when
at
first
you
come
out
from
the
city.

The dog bites and bee stings are nothing
compared to the sharp intake of breath
when another lorry puffs black
stuff from its rear into our garden,
but it blows off onto the sea.

The brave ones here swim
  in the September sea and the real men
    all year round. We wear shoes now on the beach,
      the oil is so hard to wash off,
        never mind the broken glass;
          and getting through the high grass
            can be a bit of a bugger if you're
              in a hurry   from   maybe   rain.
As for trying to run into the village
for a provision or two...forget it,
that can take two hours of talk.
Put a show on
in the local
hall and all
the advertising
will be no good
if a funeral is on.
We get Sundays off,
do nothing,
but the football matches are a pain:
the traffic,
my God,
the traffic.
Now there is talk of closing the dump in town
and bringing it back yonder
in a valley behind our hills.

Supermarket Fish

Her wanderlust shells turn up
when her father goes digging for worms.
Seeing the booty in his hands
she cries inside the window;
as a girl she'd chosen them on a beach one summer.

It rains, so she fetches him back to the house,
his bean can for worms left on the footpath,
letting the squirming things drown,
his digging fork – loose in the earth –
will have fallen by morning.

She dries his head, lets him stay
in his oil-coat that smells of distant fish,
presses a soup bowl into his earthed hands.
Then she puts a dinner on the table;
fish she bought at the supermarket,
that he thinks he caught.

Sisters at the Airport

throw arms around the years
spent on the family farm.
Visitor sister presents a package,
resident sister buys tea
and butters with tears
her mother's home-made brown bread,
fresh from Ireland.

Sr Carmella

I remember your tuning fork,
its bash by the blackboard, it taught
my mother, brother, sister,
me and my own child.
Outside school your voice stayed still
but fingers worked
a fork and trowel, making earth music.
Until the convent sold
and you moved away in your eighty-second year,
leaving the progress of the garden:
your tools breathed on, polished, packed
as if waiting for the next class to come in
for their introduction to music; life; growing.

The Fisherman's Home

His cap became a kneeler
when he blew-started the fire.
On June nights when he returned late
he still lit it, warming the walls for the night;
lit it from instinct; comfort from and for
his ancestors, knowing they needed it;
that it kept evils away.
Some nights he cooked at the fire,
toasting bread on a long fork,
boiling an egg in a bean can.
Then he would read awhile;
May to October – light fiction,
deeper literature in winter.
By two in the morning he was sleeping.

King's Cross St. Pancras

There's a Red Indian on the Victoria line,
westward bound in full regalia.
Commuters appear afraid, stare;
he's so real. Opposite him another man
in a pinstripe suit reads his Evening Standard.
He nostrils disapproval, I stifle a chuckle;
smile wide as the West, imagining *him*
                   going to work on a horse,
           shoving his briefcase in the saddlebag,
               holding an umbrella aloft,
                  answering his mobile,
             dismounting and brushing
                  dirt from his clothes.
The Red Indian takes out a Discman, briefly reads the
Red Hot Chilli Peppers CD cover credits from a HMV bag
and pops it in. I'm getting off at Seven Sisters, look
forward to my Marks & Sparks dinner and a bit of TV.

A Sunday Alone

The neighbours' pet rabbit nibbles
closer to the front wall,
elephant-like sounds of the main road
not today noise-polluting him
or me. Our greens hope for a shower
to wash the week's dust

that is inside my lungs.
Buses will cringe for space
round eight again tomorrow,
but only the odd one passes today

so I can stay in my garden,
feet on the grass,
and hear the rabbit munch.

Shop Window, Ballinasloe, 2008

When J.J. Kelso died,
his family,
closing his shop,
took some of his wares
and placed them in the window.

The shelves age, dust and dirt
gathers, ivy and other green
grows through floor cracks.

But tourists stop
and amaze at the window
with the Irish Dunlop genuine tube;
the Lucas contact set;
a fan belt in a box;
Restorio, the super car polish;
Tranco valves;
Ford spark plugs;
an advertising board for Leyland, Australia;
a Payen decarbonising set;
Duron, the finest break lines in the world;
Borg & Beck clutch plate;
Crank shaft for Austin 7 & Big 7-1936/39;
Feroda brake linings;
Sinclair radiator stop leak;
ball bearing water pump kit
and a calendar:
Esso wish all our customers
a Happy Christmas and prosperous 1951.

House-sitter

At the old woman's house
Coal-men cross the kitchen flags,
blackened hands gripping see-through plastic bags
they dump in the back kitchen. By the fire,
the old woman, her brother and me, sip tea
and grunt-greet weather reports with the men.

I am sent to fetch new coal in the scuttle,
it's too heavy so I bring it in shovel by shovel,
the last one going direct onto the fire. I vow to have
a good job when I grow up. For now I am house-sitter
to these two; front-door opener, kettle putter-onner,
egg-man, milk-cooler keeper,
the only thing I'm not allowed at is the bread knife.

Until the day I grow up when one dies before my eyes,
the other sends me running with 20p to the nearest phone box,
and I forget the instruction, whether to press button A or B.

At the wake I take the bread knife
and cut shakingly-thin slices
over and over for an endless
stream of old neighbours that come
to cry for us.

*   *   *

I didn't become a baker, or bread-van man,
or a coal-man, but stayed here;
taking the eggs from the hens,
milking the cows, as they did,
until I too am too old.

Matching the Pattern

It's years now since I've done any wallpapering.
At all the christenings,
        stations,
        Christmas-time things,
        American relations' visits,
my wallpaper stuck, unadmired.

My brother's vegetable garden,
my sisters' flower garden,
got remarks.
Sibling teases included me
as a wallflower, that it was
        appropriate:
the wallflower wallpapers.

It's just me now
        here
and though I'm unsteady with heights,
I think I'll do 'the room' again
one last time
before winter falls in
and the house will be ready for waking.

About the author

NOEL KING is a writer, actor and musician, native of Tralee, Co. Kerry. His poetry, haiku, short stories, articles and reviews have appeared in publications in over thirty countries, the poetry in journals as diverse as *Poetry Ireland Review, The Sunday Tribune, Bongos of the World* (Japan), *The Dalhousie University Review* (Canada), *Kotaz* (South Africa), *Poetry Salzburg Review* (Austria) and *Quadrant* (Australia). Along the way he has been a singer with the famous Bunratty Castle Entertainers and has worked as an arts administrator and poetry editor.

Photo: John Minihan